The Monday Morning Huddle

The Monday Morning Huddle

52 LESSONS IN BUSINESS AND LIFE

Daniel J. Cruoglio, DC

ISBN: 1534731946
ISBN 13: 9781534731943

How to Use This Book

This book is designed for you to read one lesson a week with your team or by yourself and work on implementing that lesson into your life and business. Reread it each day to assure yourself that you are getting the essence of each lesson. Answer the empowering questions at the end of each lesson. Take action each day. By the end of the year, you should be able to take yourself and/or your business from where it is now to where you want it to be. Have fun, and enjoy the process. I will see you at the top.

52 Weeks to Your Best Year Ever

1.

**"Learn to work harder on yourself
than you do on your job."
—JIM ROHN**

That was the first lesson Jim Rohn, an entrepreneur and motivational speaker, learned when he worked for Earl Shoaff, which led to his quote: "Success is not to be pursued; it to be attracted by the person you become." Even though it is important to develop the skills required for you to be better at your job, it is even more important that you take time to work on yourself. Self-development will lead you to attract massive success.

Create daily rituals for yourself. Do things on a daily basis that will improve yourself and your self-confidence. It may be mediation, exercise, reading something inspirational, changing your diet, or all of the above. Doing these things on a daily basis will begin to lay down new tracks over your old habits and create new and more empowering ones.

What did you learn from this lesson?_____

_____

_____

_____

_____

_____

What action will you take today?_____

_____

_____

_____

_____

_____

What are you grateful for after reading this lesson?_____

_____

_____

_____

_____

_____

2.

> **"It isn't the mountains ahead to climb that
> wear you out; it is the pebble in your shoe."**
> —MUHAMMAD ALI

The pebbles in your shoe are the irritants in your life. Those people, things, and situations that you allow to get under your skin create resistance and prevent you from climbing to the top of your mountain. If you are unable to withstand criticism, self-doubt, and fear, you will get worn out and quit.

Take responsibility for yourself. Know that you are doing what you were put on this earth to do. Learn to reframe whatever the irritant is to you so that it does not affect your climb. For example, if someone says to you, "What are you trying to do? It will never work," just say to yourself, "He doesn't know me, and he doesn't know what great things I am capable of doing. I am continuing my climb with enthusiasm and passion as I work my way up my mountain." Reframe every negative as a positive. Practice the skill of reframing, and watch the pebble leave your shoe.

What did you learn from this lesson?_____

_____

_____

_____

_____

_____

What action will you take today?_____

_____

_____

_____

_____

What are you grateful for after reading this lesson?_____

_____

_____

_____

_____

_____

3.

> "Don't let your fear get in the way of your biggest
> dream, even if your biggest dream is your biggest fear."
> —ANONYMOUS

When you are going for your biggest dream, only one of two things will stop you. One, your dream may not be in alignment with your values. You may have come up with that dream because you thought that is what is expected of you, or you were trying to please someone else by trying to live up to his or her values. The other is fear. Understand that fear is an illusion based on your limiting beliefs, assumptions, and perceptions.

Whenever you feel fear, ask yourself this question: "Is this thing that I am about to do going to kill me or harm me physically in any way?" If the answer is no, then face your fear, and watch it disappear.

What did you learn from this lesson?_____

_____

_____

_____

_____

_____

What action will you take today?_____

_____

_____

_____

_____

What are you grateful for after reading this lesson?_____

_____

_____

_____

_____

_____

4.

> "Keep on going, and the chances are you will stumble on something, perhaps when you are least expecting it. I never heard of anyone ever stumbling on something sitting down."
> —CHARLES F. KETTERING

Any time you put yourself out there, you are going to stumble. You have to know that if you want to carry the football, you are going to get tackled. The player sitting on the bench is safe because he is not in the game; he is watching the game. You can't stumble if you are sitting on the bench.

Get in the game. Take some action every day. Know that the stumbles and failures are part of the game. View it as feedback. Huddle up, regroup, and continue toward your goal.

What did you learn from this lesson?_____

_____

_____

_____

_____

_____

What action will you take today?_____

_____

_____

_____

_____

_____

What are you grateful for after reading this lesson?_____

_____

_____

_____

_____

_____

5.

"I want to put a ding in the universe."
—STEVE JOBS

Steve Jobs had a vision that went beyond his life. His personal mission was to put a ding in the universe. His vision proclamation for Apple was to challenge the status quo. His vision was so powerful that he got others on board who shared his vision and are carrying it out long after he is gone.

What is your vision proclamation? Come up with a vision that goes beyond your own lifetime. Create something for your family, your community, your state, and your country that will get others excited and help you achieve that vision. Meditate on it. Make it align with your values so that it inspires you to take action on a daily basis.

What did you learn from this lesson?_____

_____

_____

_____

_____

_____

What action will you take today?_____

_____

_____

_____

_____

What are you grateful for after reading this lesson?_____

_____

_____

_____

_____

_____

6.

> "It's not that I am so smart; it's that I
> just stay with problems longer."
> —ALBERT EINSTEIN

Do you quit way too soon, like the man who swam halfway across the lake and thought he couldn't make it, so he turned around and swam back? Persistence is brilliance. We all have the same possibilities as everyone else except that some people have more of a stick-to-it attitude. Never give up. Never, ever give up.

Work every day on solving the problems that come up in business and in life. It's your ability to stay with it that will allow you to come up with the proper solution.

What did you learn from this lesson?_____

_____

_____

_____

_____

_____

What action will you take today?_____

_____

_____

_____

_____

What are you grateful for after reading this lesson?_____

_____

_____

_____

_____

_____

7.

"Affirmation without action is the beginning of delusion."
—JIM ROHN

Many people think that if they say affirmations all day long, they will be able to manifest whatever that affirmation is stating. The truth is, most people don't even believe in the affirmations they are reciting to themselves. It is difficult to manifest what you do not believe and what you are not willing to take action on. Reciting affirmations without action can certainly lead to delusion, frustration, and ultimately failure.

Follow this formula: **Desire–Belief–Affirmation–Action**. This will lead to your desired result. Create affirmations, and then repeat them back to yourself. How is it resonating with you? Is it in alignment with your highest values? Do you believe it? If so, then repeat those affirmations and take the necessary actions associated with them. Then watch what happens.

Create a vision board. Let your creativity run wild, and put no limits on what you want. Cut out pictures, put them on a poster board, and look at it constantly. Spiritual entrepreneur and teacher John Assaraf ended up buying the very house he had pinned on his vision board. It can happen to you too.

What did you learn from this lesson?_____

_____

_____

_____

_____

_____

What action will you take today?_____

_____

_____

_____

_____

What are you grateful for after reading this lesson?_____

_____

_____

_____

_____

_____

8.

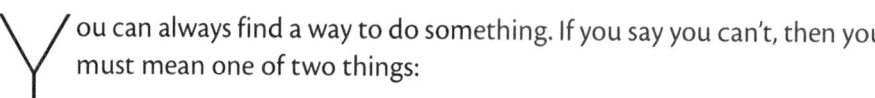

"Whether you think you can, or you think you can't—you're right."
—HENRY FORD

You can always find a way to do something. If you say you can't, then you must mean one of two things:

1. You do not know how to do it.
2. You do not want to do it.

If you do not want to, then figure out why that is the case. Is it because it is not in alignment with your values, or is it because you are afraid? If it is because it is not aligned with your values, then you should honor your values. If it is because you are afraid, then you need to work through that fear so that it dissipates and you can move forward. Develop a "can-do" attitude. You can always figure out how to do something, so never let an opportunity pass you by because you do not know how to do something. Always say yes, and figure it out later.

What did you learn from this lesson?_____

_____

_____

_____

_____

_____

What action will you take today?_____

_____

_____

_____

_____

What are you grateful for after reading this lesson?_____

_____

_____

_____

_____

_____

9.

"Yesterday's home runs don't win today's games."
—BABE RUTH

Never rest on your laurels. Every day is a new day with its own set of challenges to conquer. What worked yesterday may not work today. You must constantly keep up with your profession or business so that you do not become obsolete. It is important to stay relevant.

You should always invest in your education because knowledge is constantly changing. Put about 10 percent of your gross earnings toward sharpening your skills so that you can hit a home run today and not rely on the one you hit yesterday.

What did you learn from this lesson?_____

_____

_____

_____

_____

_____

What action will you take today?_____

_____

_____

_____

_____

What are you grateful for after reading this lesson?_____

_____

_____

_____

_____

_____

10.

> **"You miss one hundred percent of the shots you don't take."**
> **—Wayne Gretzky**

This is why it takes more than positive thinking to manifest your dreams. It requires you to take action every day. Any time you miss the opportunity to take a shot, you are guaranteed to miss—every time. Never be afraid to fail. Michael Jordon missed a lot of his last second shots, but he also made some. If he had not attempted the shots, he would have not made any. Failure is feedback. Learn from it, and take another shot.

Every night before you go to bed, review your day. See if you were able to take action steps that are getting you one step closer to your goal. You can always recalculate, but don't stop shooting.

What did you learn from this lesson?_____

_____

_____

_____

_____

_____

What action will you take today?_____

_____

_____

_____

_____

_____

What are you grateful for after reading this lesson?_____

_____

_____

_____

_____

_____

11.

> "Your most unhappy customers are your
> greatest source of learning."
> —BILL GATES

We learn more from losing than from winning. The people who have little experience with our process or product are the ones we want to get the most feedback from. These are the people who see our process differently than we do, or they may see something that is not working the way it was designed to. Never underestimate the power of a dissatisfied customer.

Create a survey form to give to your customers. Make it easy for them to tell you the truth. Make it anonymous, and ask open-ended questions (those that can't be answered with a simple yes or no) so that you can get a real sense of their experience. Remember, the customer is always right.

What did you learn from this lesson? _____

_____

_____

_____

_____

_____

What action will you take today? _____

_____

_____

_____

_____

What are you grateful for after reading this lesson? _____

_____

_____

_____

_____

_____

12.

> **"The problem with being in the rat race is
> that even if you win, you're still a rat."**
> —LILY TOMLIN

You can choose not to be a rat in the race. Constantly fighting for everything you get can be exhausting and unhealthy. There is a better way. Looking to satisfy your customer or client first and then figuring out a way for you to be satisfied as well is both rewarding and energizing.

Do your homework. Find out as much as you possibly can about your clients or customers. Find out what they need and what problems you can solve for them. Letting them know that you truly care and have their best interest at heart goes a long way, and you win in the end, too. Don't focus just on yourself and try to get as much as you can out of someone, or you will just end up being another rat in the race.

What did you learn from this lesson? _____

_____

_____

_____

_____

_____

What action will you take today? _____

_____

_____

_____

_____

_____

What are you grateful for after reading this lesson? _____

_____

_____

_____

_____

_____

13.

> "Success in business requires training and discipline and hard work. But if you're not frightened by these things, the opportunities are just as great today as they ever were."
> —DAVID ROCKEFELLER

When you implement the necessary skills and knowledge along with discipline, you begin to see opportunities all around you. It is when you are not prepared that you become victim of the circumstances that surround you. People have made huge fortunes when others panicked because they had the skills and knowledge to see the opportunities.

Always be prepared. Learn the necessary skills required to take advantage of opportunities that present themselves to you. When you are prepared, you are better able to them as opportunities rather than obstacles.

What did you learn from this lesson? _____

_____

_____

_____

_____

_____

What action will you take today? _____

_____

_____

_____

_____

_____

What are you grateful for after reading this lesson? _____

_____

_____

_____

_____

_____

14.

**"Do not wait to strike till the iron is hot;
but make it hot by striking."
—WILLIAM B. SPRAGUE**

How many times do we prevent ourselves from taking action because we feel it is not the right time? The fact is that it will never be the right time. Creating constant action toward your goal or objective will produce feedback that you can use to move yourself forward. Having a fear of mediocrity will hold you back. It fosters procrastination and thus prevents you from moving forward. Don't be afraid to fail. Look at it as a learning process, and move forward with your new knowledge.

Make it a point to go out every day and fail. Do something that will challenge you. Learn from it, and move forward. The more you fail, the faster you will succeed.

What did you learn from this lesson? _____

_____

_____

_____

_____

_____

What action will you take today? _____

_____

_____

_____

_____

What are you grateful for after reading this lesson? _____

_____

_____

_____

_____

15.

"The definition of insanity is doing the same thing over and over again and expecting different results."
—ALBERT EINSTEIN

I am sure you have heard this quote before, and even if you have, you may still find yourself repeating the same patterns of behavior over and over again. When you take action and your action does not get you your desired result, then you must change what you are doing, or you will end up with the same result. People are creatures of habit, and if we do not change our habits, we will continually be chasing our tails. Don't drive yourself crazy by doing the same things and expecting that things are going to change. They will not.

For every action, there is a result. By being conscious of your actions, you have the ability to analyze the result, make the necessary changes to an action, and create a new action. That new action will produce a different result. Keep doing that until you get the result you desire.

What did you learn from this lesson? _____

_____

_____

_____

_____

_____

What action will you take today? _____

_____

_____

_____

_____

What are you grateful for after reading this lesson? _____

_____

_____

_____

_____

_____

16.

**"Whatever the mind of man can conceive
and believe, it can achieve."
—NAPOLEON HILL**

t is amazing that we have a power to convert a thought into physical exis-
tence. All of the innovation we have seen over the years has been a direct
result of the vision people had to create and change the world. People like
Disney, Jobs, Gates, and others held a vision in their minds for so long that it
actually began to manifest on the physical plane and change the way the world
operates.

Take time to visualize. Set time aside to be alone without any distractions,
and imagine what you would like to achieve. Then hold on to that thought
until it begins to manifest. Holding on to the thought is what creates the
magic. The power comes in holding on to that thought when people will tell
you it can't be done or that you are not capable of doing it. Never letting
that thought go is the secret to achieving the very vision you created in your
mind's eye.

What did you learn from this lesson? _____

_____

_____

_____

_____

_____

What action will you take today? _____

_____

_____

_____

_____

_____

What are you grateful for after reading this lesson? _____

_____

_____

_____

_____

_____

17.

"Be thankful for what you have; you'll end up having more. If you concentrate on what you don't have, you will never, ever have enough."
—OPRAH WINFREY

When you are grateful and focus on what you have, the universe will supply you with more. The opposite is also true. When you focus on lack and not having enough, guess what? The universe provides you with more lack. Understanding the power of gratitude can give you the things you seek because you appreciate everything that has been given to you so far. Every experience is a blessing. If you can see the blessing, then you can more forward, if you don't see the blessing, then you end up getting the very things you say you don't want.

Every night before you go to sleep, take out a journal and write down what you were grateful for that day. Begin to see the blessings in every situation. Begin to see how each event is moving you closer to your dreams by making you into the person who attracts what you have been dreaming about.

What did you learn from this lesson? _____

_____

_____

_____

_____

_____

What action will you take today? _____

_____

_____

_____

_____

_____

What are you grateful for after reading this lesson? _____

_____

_____

_____

_____

_____

18.

"Never put off till tomorrow what you can do today."
—Thomas Jefferson

Procrastination can come from a variety of different sources, but each has an underlying fear associated with it. It could be the fear of mediocrity or risk or failure or success or rejection. Whatever it is, you must face it so that it will dissipate. Know that the fear you are experiencing is not going to harm you, and then move forward and get it done today. You will be surprised at how quickly you can attain your desired goal by facing your fear and avoiding procrastination.

Create a to-do list each night before your retire to bed. Then, at the end of each day, review your list to see which items you accomplished and which items did not get done. If you ended up doing all the easy tasks and did not get around to doing the harder and probably the more important tasks, then some fear is associated with that task. An adage in the South says, "If you have to swallow a frog, it is best not to stare at it for a long time." Eat your big frog first, and you will feel better about yourself. And procrastination will no longer hold you back.

What did you learn from this lesson? _____

_____

_____

_____

_____

_____

What action will you take today? _____

_____

_____

_____

_____

What are you grateful for after reading this lesson? _____

_____

_____

_____

_____

_____

19.

> "Far better it is to dare mighty things, to win glorious
> triumphs, even though checkered by failure...
> than to rank with those poor spirits who neither
> enjoy nor suffer much because they live in a gray
> twilight that knows not victory nor defeat."
> —THEODORE ROOSEVELT

t is much better to have tried something and fail than to never have tried it at all. Most people live with regret because they never went for the brass ring. You were not put on this earth to be a spectator; you were put on this earth to be an active participant in creating a life that will enhance the lives of others. We live in a country and a time of true opportunity. It is almost impossible to fail if we follow our hearts and put in the time and effort required to make it happen.

Create your bucket list. No holds barred. Then plan on doing each activity, one at a time, and checking each one off along the way. Your life will be better for the attempt.

What did you learn from this lesson? _____

_____

_____

_____

_____

_____

What action will you take today? _____

_____

_____

_____

_____

_____

What are you grateful for after reading this lesson? _____

_____

_____

_____

_____

_____

20.

"The successful man is the one who finds out what is the matter with his business before his competitors do."
—ROY L. SMITH

Never take your business for granted. Always keep your finger on the pulse of your business. Know your numbers, check your process and systems, and make sure your people have the same vision as you and your company. Never stay stagnant. You should always be reinventing yourself to keep up with the changing times. When was the last time you saw a pay phone on a street corner? If you don't make the necessary changes, someone else will.

Every quarter, you and your team should do a SWOT analysis (strengths, weaknesses, opportunities, and threats). Take at least half a day to work through each one, and then come up with a plan to optimize your strengths and opportunities and to minimize your weaknesses and threats. It will keep your business fresh and up-to-date.

What did you learn from this lesson? _____

_____

_____

_____

_____

_____

What action will you take today? _____

_____

_____

_____

_____

What are you grateful for after reading this lesson? _____

_____

_____

_____

_____

_____

21.

**"Many of life's failures are people who did not realize
how close they were to success when they gave up."
—Thomas Edison**

Appropriate here is the quote mentioned earlier about the man who swam halfway across the lake and thought he could not make it, so he swam back. When you do not have a clear vision, it is difficult to see how close you were to actually succeeding. You have not failed at anything unless you give up. So never give up.

This is why it so important to create your vision board, as mentioned earlier. Add to it or change it as you see fit, but never neglect it. Remember, John Assaraf bought the very house that he put on his vision board.

What did you learn from this lesson? _____

_____

_____

_____

_____

_____

What action will you take today? _____

_____

_____

_____

_____

_____

What are you grateful for after reading this lesson? _____

_____

_____

_____

_____

_____

22.

"A calm sea does not make a skilled sailor."
—AFRICAN PROVERB

Anyone can be the captain of a boat when the waters are calm, but you cannot learn anything when conditions are perfect. It is when you are challenged by the waves and currents that your skills are tested and you are stretched beyond your apparent abilities so that you become a skilled sailor. The rougher the waters, the more skill required to manage your ship. Don't be afraid to challenge yourself. You will grow from it, and the results will follow.

Make it a point to fail every day. Don't play it safe. Look at failure as feedback. Learn from it, and never attach it to your self-esteem. All the greats became great because they failed more than anyone else. Failure is the stepping stone you need to grow. Remember, it is difficult to climb a smooth mountain. Get out there and dig in, and watch your growth begin.

What did you learn from this lesson? _____

_____

_____

_____

_____

_____

What action will you take today? _____

_____

_____

_____

_____

What are you grateful for after reading this lesson? _____

_____

_____

_____

_____

_____

23.

> **"No problem can be solved with the same
> level of consciousness that created it."**
> —ALBERT EINSTEIN

When a problem arises, it generally comes from a place of low vibrational energy. To try to solve a problem in the same vibration in which it arose is fruitless because you are generally in a state of survival, where your options are limited. You must raise your energy to a higher vibrational state to access more options and solve the problem at a much higher level.

State the problem before you go to sleep, and allow your higher vibration to take over while you rest and you are in a nonjudgmental and nonattracted state. You will be surprised when you wake up to find the answer that solves the problem. Be open-minded, and allow yourself to think outside the box.

What did you learn from this lesson? _____

_____

_____

_____

_____

_____

What action will you take today? _____

_____

_____

_____

_____

_____

What are you grateful for after reading this lesson? _____

_____

_____

_____

_____

_____

24.

"Knowledge is not power; application
of knowledge is power."
—JOHN ASSARAF

A lot of people are motivated underachievers. They read all the books, go to all the seminars, and take all the courses, yet they do not apply what they have learned. It becomes more entertainment than knowledge.

Take what you learn and implement only one thing at a time until all of it is completed. Taking small steps prevents you from feeling overwhelmed, and over time, you will be converting all that you learned into real knowledge and power.

What did you learn from this lesson? _____

_____

_____

_____

_____

What action will you take today? _____

_____

_____

_____

_____

What are you grateful for after reading this lesson? _____

_____

_____

_____

_____

_____

25.

"The measure of a great leader is not how he treats
his peers; it is how he treats his subordinates."
—UNKNOWN

M any successful people make it a habit to treat everyone equally. The doorman, the waiter, the housekeeper, and the messenger are no different than other executives. Treat everyone with the respect and dignity they each deserve.

Make it a habit to be kind to everyone you come in contact with on a daily basis. Remember that each person, whether he or she does something right or not, is still deserving of love. You are no better or worse than anyone else. Show an attitude of gratitude, and watch your self-worth increase.

What did you learn from this lesson? _____

_____

_____

_____

_____

What action will you take today? _____

_____

_____

_____

_____

What are you grateful for after reading this lesson? _____

_____

_____

_____

_____

_____

26.

> **"Wisdom is the instantaneous recognition
> that crisis is a blessing."**
> **Dr. John DeMartini**

nderstand that every experience in your life is purposeful and is designed to help you grow. Know that life does not happen to you but rather is a gift you should be grateful for. For a lobster to grow, it must shed its shell, which was pressing against its flesh, and become vulnerable until it is able to grow another shell. Each time you shed a layer of yourself, it will be uncomfortable, and you will be vulnerable until it becomes comfortable again. To continue to grow, you must shed another layer. Wisdom comes from understanding that everything that was once viewed as a crisis is actually another opportunity for you to grow. Open yourself up to this idea, and you will become the master of your life.

Each night, spend five to ten minutes reflecting on the day. Be grateful for all that has happened to you, and learn from every experience without judgment. In the morning, you will wake up renewed so that every margining becomes a new birthday.

What did you learn from this lesson? _____

_____

_____

_____

_____

_____

What action will you take today? _____

_____

_____

_____

_____

_____

What are you grateful for after reading this lesson? _____

_____

_____

_____

_____

_____

27.

> "When times are tough, a client will
> leave you, but a friend won't."
> —Dr. Ivan Misner

Networking is defined as developing and maintaining contacts and personal connections with a variety of people who might be helpful to you and your career. Learning how to network effectively is one of the most powerful tools an individual can use to advance his or her personal and professional life. Networking boils down to building real relationships, actively maintaining them, and giving as much as you take. I have coined the phrase "Dating for Dollars." Networking is finding people whom you never met before and turning them into friends forever.

Never take the hunting approach in networking. I am sure you have been at events where you meet people, and all they want to do is try to sell you their product or service. Then you see them at another event, and what do you do? You try to avoid them. Whenever someone is hunting, the thing they are hunting is running away from them.

Be a fisherman. When you fish, you drop your line, and the fish come to you. Build sincere relationships in which you can create mutual benefit. Never, ever ask for anything from someone unless you have developed an affinity with them. A good way to start is by thinking of ways to help them. You want to be known as the person people can come to when they need something. That is good karma.

And finally, remember FU—the follow-up.

Don't ever get someone's business card or e-mail address and forget about it. Find ways to stay in touch. Maintain your network. Whenever you find an article that might be of interest to them, send it their way. Keep track of their birthday and mark it on your calendar. Send birthday cards to everyone you know, along with a nice note to let them know you have not forgotten about them and that you do not want them to forget you. Ultimately, a network can be an investment with the benefits that outweigh the costs. Just stick to it, and watch your network increase your net worth.

What did you learn from this lesson? _____

_____

_____

_____

_____

_____

What action will you take today? _____

_____

_____

_____

_____

What are you grateful for after reading this lesson? _____

_____

_____

_____

_____

_____

28.

"When it's fun, you'll get it done."
—Dr. Dan Cruoglio

Your brain is wired for survival. As human beings, we have three brains:

1. The *neocortex* is the newest brain; it allows us to think and create ideas.
2. The *limbic* brain is responsible for how we feel.
3. The *reptilian* brain is the instinctive brain.

Because the primary function of the brain is survival, some of our thoughts can evoke fear and prevent us from moving forward. As humans, we are motivated by pain and pleasure. We tend to move away from pain and toward pleasure. Keeping this in mind, it is important to know that we will avoid anything we perceive to be painful, and we will pursue anything we perceive as pleasurable. That's why when we get overwhelmed, we tend to get distracted and look for things that are pleasurable and avoid the tasks we think are painful.

Solution: Figure out a way to make the tasks that you have been avoiding fun. For example, you may find exercise boring but you find basketball enjoyable. You can run up and down the court shooting baskets having fun and still get your exercise. You may find losing weight to be challenging. You can make it fun by creating low-calorie versions of your favorite foods that still taste good. No matter what the task, you can always find a way to make it fun. When your brain perceives it to be fun, you will definitely get it done.

What did you learn from this lesson? _____

_____

_____

_____

_____

_____

What action will you take today? _____

_____

_____

_____

_____

_____

What are you grateful for after reading this lesson? _____

_____

_____

_____

_____

_____

29.

"Any man who can drive safely while kissing a pretty girl is simply not giving the kiss the attention it deserves."
—ALBERT EINSTEIN

Have you ever tried multitasking, or trying to do more than one thing at the same time? Well, it is simply impossible to multitask. What is actually happening is that you are switching from one task to the next. When this happens, your brain has to leave one task and focus on the other, paying no attention to the previous task. This practice can lead to a decrease in productivity, and ultimately it becomes a time waster.

Try reciting the alphabet as fast as you can. Pretty easy. Now count from one to twenty-six as fast as you can. Also easy. Now try multitasking by doing them both at the same time. You are actually switching back and forth: A, 1, 2, B, 3, C, and so forth. Pretty slow, huh? In reality, it actually slows you down. So focus on one task at a time, and if you ever have the opportunity to kiss a pretty girl, for God's sake, pull the car over.

What did you learn from this lesson? _____

_____

_____

_____

_____

_____

What action will you take today? _____

_____

_____

_____

_____

What are you grateful for after reading this lesson? _____

_____

_____

_____

_____

30.

"Only the man who is not hungry says the coconut has a hard shell."
—ETHIOPIAN PROVERB

How hungry are you to succeed? What are you willing to sacrifice in the short term to receive something in the long term? Most people go through life just satisfied to get by. They are afraid to break through their internal thermostat and reach greater heights. When your voice of inspiration on the inside is louder than all the voices you hear on the outside, then you will do whatever it takes to succeed.

You were born for greatness. Everything you need is already there and sits dormant inside you, waiting for you to come to the realization that you are awesome. Find out what truly inspires you to tears, and then go out there and crack open some coconuts.

What did you learn from this lesson? _____

_____

_____

_____

_____

_____

What action will you take today? _____

_____

_____

_____

_____

_____

What are you grateful for after reading this lesson? _____

_____

_____

_____

_____

_____

31.

> **"It's not rejection; it's redirection."**
> **—COURTNEY TURNER**

One of the biggest fears business owners face is the fear of rejection. Most people don't even realize that it is a fear at all. The need to make someone else happy and to seek approval can take you away from your own purpose and desires. Learning to discipline yourself to set boundaries and to avoid taking things so personally can give you the inner strength you need to turn it all around.

When someone says no to you, it is not about you. One of the things you can do is start saying no to other people rather than trying to please everyone to gain a false sense of approval or validation. Self-confidence and resilience are common traits among leaders. When you can become free of guilt and have little or no need for approval, you will be redirected and can begin to attract your ideal clients and customers.

What did you learn from this lesson? _____

_____

_____

_____

_____

What action will you take today? _____

_____

_____

_____

_____

What are you grateful for after reading this lesson? _____

_____

_____

_____

_____

_____

32.

**"Knowledge is learning something every day.
Wisdom is letting go of something every day."**
—ZEN PROVERB

Learning something every day gives us the knowledge to become more competent, and as a result of that competence, we become more confident. Letting go of something every day allows us to stop carrying around the baggage of our past and focus our intentions on the present moment so that our past no longer has to define us. We are free to be whatever we choose to be. Let this knowledge give you wisdom, and start letting go.

What did you learn from this lesson? _____

_____

_____

_____

_____

_____

What action will you take today? _____

_____

_____

_____

_____

What are you grateful for after reading this lesson? _____

_____

_____

_____

_____

_____

33.

> **"I've learned that people will forget what you said, people will forget what you did, but people will never forget how you made them feel."**
> **—MAYA ANGELOU**

Getting someone to remember you is not a matter of saying something clever or intelligent, nor is it an act or deed that you thought was admirable. It is the way you made them feel after the words and deeds are long forgotten. It is the intention behind every word and deed that people pick up on, whether it is something that warms their heart or gets their goat. Your intention is the key to your success or failure in life or in business.

Words said with different intentions can be perceived in different ways. When you come from a place of "What's in it for me?" that vibration is sent out and picked up by others. However, when you come from a place of "How can I be of service to you?" that vibration is also sent out and received. Each vibration creates a feeling that is long lasting. It's all up to you. So put your attention on your intention, and you will be remembered fondly.

What did you learn from this lesson? _____

_____

_____

_____

_____

_____

What action will you take today? _____

_____

_____

_____

_____

What are you grateful for after reading this lesson? _____

_____

_____

_____

_____

_____

34.

**"Obstacles are those frightful things you see
when you take your eyes off your goal."**
—HENRY FORD

How clear are your goals, and how badly do you want them? Having a crystal-clear vision of your goals allows you to see past everything that might stand in your way. When American swimmer Florence Chadwick made one of her attempts to swim the English Channel, it was very cold and foggy. At one point in her swim, she asked to be pulled from the water because the cold water, the fog, and the jellyfish were too much for her to handle. When they finally pulled her from the water and warmed her up, her coach told her that she was only a quarter of a mile from shore when they pulled her out. Florence told her coach that if she could have only been able to see the shore, she would have kept swimming.

When you don't have a clear vision and a true purpose that is greater than yourself, you allow fear and obstacles to get in the way. Make your goals big and clear, and watch all your obstacles disappear.

What did you learn from this lesson? _____

_____

_____

_____

_____

_____

What action will you take today? _____

_____

_____

_____

_____

_____

What are you grateful for after reading this lesson? _____

_____

_____

_____

_____

_____

35.

> **"Time is money."**
> **—BENJAMIN FRANKLIN**

One of the things I find interesting is how people have different beliefs around money. I remember reading a book in which personal-development guru Dan Millman says he was watching an episode of the show *Lifestyles of the Rich and Famous* in which they were taking a tour of Barbara Streisand's home. In one room of her home, she had a beautiful rug with a beautiful design that covered the whole room. When she lifted the rug up, underneath was the same design in her marble floor so that when she had the rug cleaned, she could still enjoy the design. At the time, Millman thought that such a display of wealth was "ostentatious and offensive."

He writes that at that moment, he was unaware of his own negative associations, prejudice, and naïve judgments until he did some self-reflection that made him aware that he was passing judgment on someone he did not even know. He later found out that Barbara Streisand donated and raised more money for charities in one year than most people earn in a lifetime. He goes on to admit that at the time, he was struggling financially.

What beliefs do you have around money? Have your beliefs held you back from achieving the financial goals that you have set for yourself? Start by figuring out what your time is worth. I always ask my clients, would you pay your fee to go to you? Money forces you to confront your self- worth. Once you confront your fears, you can begin to attract those clients who truly value the goods and services that you provide. This increases the level of energy and creates a win-win situation. When you think about it, all money is, is Energy.

What did you learn from this lesson? _____

_____

_____

_____

_____

_____

What action will you take today? _____

_____

_____

_____

_____

_____

What are you grateful for after reading this lesson? _____

_____

_____

_____

_____

_____

36.

"A candle loses nothing by lighting another candle."
—B. J. PALMER

as someone who is of the same profession as you ever asked you for help and you were hesitant to oblige because you felt you would lose some type of competitive edge? Well, the opposite is true. Helping someone else enrich his or her life with your knowledge and expertise only enhances your life. Your life is not about keeping things to yourself but rather sharing them with the world. The best way to get more of what you want is to give what you want away. You want more recognition? Then give more recognition to others. You want more love? Then give more love. You want more money? Then invest more money.

The more you give, the more you receive. This may seem counterintuitive, but it is founded in the universal laws of life. So never be afraid to light someone else's candle. Doing so will not deplete your light but rather allow your light to shine more brightly. So light up the world today, and see what happens!

What did you learn from this lesson? _____

_____

_____

_____

_____

_____

What action will you take today? _____

_____

_____

_____

_____

What are you grateful for after reading this lesson? _____

_____

_____

_____

_____

_____

37.

"Believe nothing, no matter where you have read it, or who has said it, no matter if I have said it, unless it agrees with your own reason and your own common sense."
—BUDDHA

Don't let UFOs (unidentified foreign opinions) invade your brain. When did someone's opinion of you become more important than your own? As self-help author Wayne Dyer said, "Other people's opinions of me are none of my business." Don't let someone's opinion of you dictate how you feel. I remember when I was younger and people would say to me, "Do you know your hair is turning gray?" This used to bother me until I accepted it, and then it had no power over me. Now that I have no hair, I wish people would say that to me.

Start driving your own bus. Don't give up your authority to someone else. No one knows you better than you. Be aware of your words and how you speak about yourself. Words are powerful because they come from your being that produces a frequency that produces your thoughts, and those thoughts produce your words. Your words produce your actions, and your actions produce your results. So if you don't like your results, start showing up differently, and drive your own bus because if you don't, someone else will.

What did you learn from this lesson? _____

_____

_____

_____

_____

_____

What action will you take today? _____

_____

_____

_____

_____

_____

What are you grateful for after reading this lesson? _____

_____

_____

_____

_____

_____

38.

**"A friendship founded on business is better
than a business founded on friendship."
—JOHN D. ROCKEFELLER**

Whenever you decide to build a business, make sure you hire the best people who will help you achieve your goals and objectives so that your vision and mission can become a reality. Successful business-people know the importance of hiring people who are smarter than them, especially if they are smarter in areas of their weaknesses. Nonsavvy business-people will hire people who are not as smart as them because they either want to feel as if they are in control or they want to feel important. Other times, they will hire their friends because they thought it was a good idea at the time.

One of the three foundations of building a successful business is *probability*. Any decision you make must answer this question: "What is the probability that this decision will move my business in the direction I envision?" With that information, you can hire the best people first and become friends later.

What did you learn from this lesson? _____

_____

_____

_____

_____

_____

What action will you take today? _____

_____

_____

_____

_____

_____

What are you grateful for after reading this lesson? _____

_____

_____

_____

_____

_____

39.

> **"We must be willing to get rid of the life we've planned so as to have the life that is waiting for us."**
> **—JOSEPH CAMPBELL**

There is an expression that says, "You plan, and God laughs." Your life is a series of adventures designed to help you find your true bliss. Every dragon we slay brings us closer to our true selves as we begin to discover the valuable, bright, shining stars that we are when we entered this world. Unfortunately, that star got covered up every time we allowed ourselves to be influenced by our parents, teachers, clergy, etc. When we grow up, we can hardly recognize that star because it has been covered up, until something happens to us and we are forced to deal with it.

When we build up the courage to deal with a situation (divorce, bankruptcy, a death etc.), a piece of the covering falls away, and we begin to see the light shining out from our stars. As we remove the covering, it is then that we realize we are that bright, shining star. Follow your bliss, and let your life shine!

What did you learn from this lesson? _____

_____

_____

_____

_____

_____

What action will you take today? _____

_____

_____

_____

_____

_____

What are you grateful for after reading this lesson? _____

_____

_____

_____

_____

_____

40.

**"The world breaks everyone, and afterward,
many are strong at the broken places."
—ERNEST HEMINGWAY**

Have you ever broken a bone? They say that when you break a bone and it heals, the place where the break occurred is much stronger. So too can it be in life and business. If you ever want to attain a certain level of success, you must be willing to fail massively. We were born with a human spirit that is more resilient than anything man can make on his own. It is just that we forget how strong and powerful we are, and we allow the stepping stones that will lead us to success to be a tombstone and a dead end. Those who recognize that failure is only feedback and is not attached to their self-esteem are the ones who thrive, while others who wallow in self-pity allow those events to crush their dreams.

Being resilient means to become successful again, even after bad things happen. We have that ability. It was given to us at birth, but some of us forget that we possess it. Here is a fact: the world will break you. It will knock you down and try to crush you, but if you remember that you are resilient, then those places that were broken become much stronger, and you are much better as a result of that happening. So break a leg!

What did you learn from this lesson? _____

_____

_____

_____

_____

_____

What action will you take today? _____

_____

_____

_____

_____

_____

What are you grateful for after reading this lesson? _____

_____

_____

_____

_____

_____

41.

"If the only prayer you said in your life was 'thank you,' that would suffice."
—Meister Eckhart

Whenever we judge an experience in a way that it creates an unbalanced perception of reality, we create emotions. Whether you become infatuated with someone or something or you try to impose yourself on someone or something, it can only create an imbalance that leads to negativity, frustration, and chaos. However, when you are grateful for the experience, instead of walking through life with a ball and chain around your ankle, you can use that experience as rocket fuel to propel you to the next level of your life or business in a way that creates support, order, and peace.

In truth, the only two true emotions that exist are love and gratitude. So when you say "Thank you" for every experience, you will find yourself being propelled to the next level. Take on the attitude of gratitude, and watch what happens.

What did you learn from this lesson? _____

_____

_____

_____

_____

_____

What action will you take today? _____

_____

_____

_____

_____

_____

What are you grateful for after reading this lesson? _____

_____

_____

_____

_____

_____

42.

"Here is the test to find whether your mission on earth is finished: if you're alive, it isn't."
—RICHARD BACH

This past week, I lost my mom. Today, as you are reading this, we are bringing her to her final resting place. My mom was the ultimate care giver. Her mission in life was to take care of others. She did it well. She innately knew that life was about helping others without any regard for self. That service to others was her ultimate reward in life. Her highest value was taking care of other people. She honored that value throughout her life, and it brought her a lifetime of friendships, from the poorest of poor to the richest of rich. It didn't matter to Mom who you were or what your status in life was; she treated everyone the same.

My mom cannot take another breath. Her mission is complete. She has given me that gift of helping others, and I intend to fulfill that mission as well. What is your mission? What were you put on this earth to do? You were given a gift from God. What you do with that it is your gift to him. Honor your values. By doing so, you will find a lifetime of fulfillment. When you try to live up to someone else's values or try to impose your values on someone else, that makes you unhappy and frustrated. You have a mission. As long as you can take that deep breath, your mission in life is not yet complete. Find it. Honor it. Live it.

What did you learn from this lesson? _____

_____

_____

_____

_____

_____

What action will you take today? _____

_____

_____

_____

_____

_____

What are you grateful for after reading this lesson? _____

_____

_____

_____

_____

_____

43.

> "In the end, we only regret the chances we didn't take, the relationships we were afraid to have, and the decisions we waited too long to make."
> —Lewis Carroll

What would you do if you knew you couldn't fail? Life is too short to play the woulda–shoulda game. Imagine yourself sitting in your rocking chair looking back on your life. What were the things you wished you had done or attempted but were too afraid to start? Those of us who have tried many things know that everything doesn't work out the way we want it to sometimes, but the fact that we attempted it makes us feel a lot better than never doing it at all.

So go after whatever you want with no attachment to the outcome, and you will find that the satisfaction is in the journey, not the destination. Live your life with no regrets, and watch what happens.

What did you learn from this lesson? _____

_____

_____

_____

_____

What action will you take today? _____

_____

_____

_____

_____

What are you grateful for after reading this lesson? _____

_____

_____

_____

_____

_____

44.

**"Success in life is the result of good judgment.
Good judgment is the result of experience.
Experience is often the result of bad judgment."**
—ANTHONY ROBBINS

Success comes about by learning from our experiences and moving forward in a positive direction. Life is not a proving ground; it is a learning ground. When we experience something, we should take away the lesson rather than judge it as good or bad. The moment that we judge an experience as bad, it becomes a mistake. Without judgment, it is only an experience in which we now have an opportunity to learn. So when you judge less and learn more, success will be the result of your right action.

What did you learn from this lesson? _____

_____

_____

_____

_____

_____

What action will you take today? _____

_____

_____

_____

_____

_____

What are you grateful for after reading this lesson? _____

_____

_____

_____

_____

_____

45.

**"The greatest use of life is to spend it for
something that will outlast it."
—WILLIAM JAMES**

Our greatest purpose in life is to create a vision that will last beyond our lifetimes. In 1960, President Kennedy had a vision that man would go to the moon and returned safely to earth before the end of the decade. That vision motivated men to work on accomplishing that mission. In 1969, that vision of President Kennedy was made a reality, long after his death.

What do you want to do to leave your mark on this planet? To accomplish it, you must have a vision that is greater than yourself and extends well beyond your lifetime. It is your life; spend it wisely.

What did you learn from this lesson? _____

_____

_____

_____

_____

_____

What action will you take today? _____

_____

_____

_____

_____

_____

What are you grateful for after reading this lesson? _____

_____

_____

_____

_____

_____

46.

"The more you lose yourself in something greater than yourself, the more energy you will have."
—NORMAN VINCENT PEALE

The day you realize that it is not about you is the day the world becomes your oyster. Creating a vision of something greater than yourself will not only empower you; it will also energize you to succeed. Bill Gates was not concerned about what people thought when he had a vision of a computer in every household. His passion and drive for something outside of himself provided the energy to manifest his dream.

Here are three ways to raise your energy:

1. **Judge less.** How you judge yourself and others as well as the world can hold you back and lower your energy.
2. **Love more.** When you love more, judgment automatically lessens, and fear dissolves, while your energy rises.
3. **Lose yourself in something greater than yourself.** Once you connect with an idea or cause that is greater than yourself, your passion and drive will create more energy to manifest your vision.

Now, go on. Start standing for something bigger than yourself, and watch the world become your oyster.

What did you learn from this lesson? _____

_____

_____

_____

_____

_____

What action will you take today? _____

_____

_____

_____

_____

_____

What are you grateful for after reading this lesson? _____

_____

_____

_____

_____

_____

47.

"You can easily judge the character of a man by how
he treats those who can do nothing for him."
—JOHANN WOLFGANG VON GOETHE

t is not how we treat our peers that is important but how we treat our subordinates. That reveals who we truly are. Every single human being who walks the face of this earth is worthy of love, no matter what he or she has or hasn't done for us. Successful CEOs know the importance of treating everyone in their company with the utmost respect and dignity, whether they are top executives or line workers.

How do you treat everyone you come in contact with on a daily basis? Do you treat them with kindness? With distain? Or are you just indifferent? Knowing the answer to those questions can make a huge difference in your life and in the life of your business.

What did you learn from this lesson? _____

_____

_____

_____

_____

_____

What action will you take today? _____

_____

_____

_____

_____

_____

What are you grateful for after reading this lesson? _____

_____

_____

_____

_____

_____

48.

> "Our number one priority is company culture. Our belief is that if you get the culture right, most of the other stuff—like great customer service, or building a great long-term enduring brand, or passionate employees and customers—will happen naturally on its own."
> —TONY HSIEH, CEO, ZAPPOS

What's your culture like? One of my best customer-service experiences was ordering shoes from Zappos. They allow you to return anything you want, no questions asked, and even pay for the return shipping. I even once asked for a discount on some very expensive shoes, and the representative gave me the family discount. You think I am going to order from them again? Absolutely! One of the most important things in any business is to get the culture right. Nothing is worse than speaking to a representative who is there only to collect a paycheck and does the bare minimum. There are actually people out there who love talking to and helping people. They would do it for free if they could. Those are the ones you want operating the front line of your business.

Sometimes we get so caught up in filling a vacancy that our only requirement is that the person has a pulse. First you have to figure out what you want the culture of your company to be, based on your values and the values you want your company to exhibit. Then you have to find people who are in alignment with those values, and everything will fall into place naturally. So if your culture allows for rude, unfriendly, and caustic people who cannot smile while on the phone or look you in the eye when in your presence, then it's time to create a new culture, or you will wonder why you cannot create consumer loyalty.

What did you learn from this lesson? _____

_____

_____

_____

_____

What action will you take today? _____

_____

_____

_____

_____

What are you grateful for after reading this lesson? _____

_____

_____

_____

_____

49.

"If you ain't the lead dog, the view never changes."
—LEWIS GRIZZARD

Are you managing or leading your life? When you are *managing* your life, you are maintaining things just as they are, making sure everything gets done so that you don't lose any ground. When you are *leading* your life, you are looking to improve yourself from where you are to where you want to be. As human beings, we are motivated in only two ways: by the prospect of gain or the prevention of pain. Any time we do something to keep us from suffering any horrible consequence, we are motivated by pain prevention. When we look to do tasks that will move us forward, then we are motivated by the prospect of gain.

Managing your life requires you to do things to prevent pain so that you don't move backward. *Leading* your life requires you to do the tasks that are not urgent but will move you forward because of what you will gain from doing them. Only you can do those activities that will move your business and life forward. All the other stuff that needs to be managed can be delegated out to the people who have the necessary skill sets to perform them and the values that align with your company's culture. So be a leader, and see if you can manage your life and watch the view change.

What did you learn from this lesson? _____

_____

_____

_____

_____

_____

What action will you take today? _____

_____

_____

_____

_____

_____

What are you grateful for after reading this lesson? _____

_____

_____

_____

_____

_____

50.

> **"We are our choices."**
> **—JEAN-PAUL SARTRE**

Have you ever wondered why you are where you are today? It is all a series of choices that you made up until this point. Sometimes we forget that not making a choice is also a choice and that inaction can stymie your growth. The first step is to identify what it is you really want; be as specific as you can. A friend of mine, Jill, recently wrote on Facebook that she prayed that she wanted to feel like a teenager again and woke up with a zit on her chin. So make sure that your first step is to be as clear and specific as possible about what you want.

The next step is to ask yourself empowering questions that will lead you to the answers you need to make the correct choices. If you ask unempowering questions like "Why me?" or "Why does this always happen to me?" then you will get the answer. That answer will lead you to a series of choices that will limit your growth by fostering more of what you don't want. Ask yourself empowering questions like "What steps do I need to take to get where I want to be?" and "What skills do I need to learn to help me get there?" The answers will lead to a series of choices that take you where you really want to go to.

Sometimes we allow fear and doubt to seep into our choices because our focus is on ourselves rather than on what we really want. Once you create the vision of what you really want and make the choices necessary to attain it, you will find that you will really like the person you have become because of the choices you made.

What did you learn from this lesson? _____

_____

_____

_____

_____

_____

What action will you take today? _____

_____

_____

_____

_____

What are you grateful for after reading this lesson? _____

_____

_____

_____

_____

51.

"No man is an island."
—JOHN DONNE

Have you ever thought that you can run a successful business on your own? Well, think again. Human beings do not thrive when isolated from others. We are all part of the orchestra of life. When one person tries to play all the parts, it can only lead to burnout and failure. Recognizing that your success is dependent on the team you build and the team you lead is the first step to taking your business to the next level. When the whole team is greater than the sum of its parts, it creates a synergy that is unstoppable. Creating your team requires you to find people who are in alignment with your values and the values of your company and who respect you as a leader. People don't want to be managed; they want to be led.

As the leader, you are the conductor of the orchestra that will produce the harmony and the rhythms that will catapult your business and allow it to grow. So don't think you can do it on your own, or you will find yourself alone on the island of regret.

What did you learn from this lesson? _____

_____

_____

_____

_____

_____

What action will you take today? _____

_____

_____

_____

_____

What are you grateful for after reading this lesson? _____

_____

_____

_____

_____

_____

52.

> **"Everyone has the will to win, but not everyone has the will to prepare to win."**
> **—Bobby Knight**

D o you prepare to win? What do you do each day that prepares you to be the best at what you do? What daily rituals have you incorporated into your life that make you the very best in your field? John Wooden, who led UCLA to ten consecutive college basketball championships, taught his players how to put on their socks properly so that they would not get blisters.

How detailed are you in your preparation? Winners do what losers are not willing to do. That's why there is no traffic on the extra mile. Where is your focus? Is it on the outcome, or is it on the process? If it is on the outcome, then you will create actions and behaviors that you do consistently to get you from where you are now to where you want to go. If you are focused on the process, then the minute that things get tough or uncomfortable, you will quit. Preparation is the key to winning. Daily rituals such as meditation, exercise, reading, and writing are staples to any preparation. How much do you value yourself? Do you invest in yourself by hiring a coach and going to seminars and workshops, or do you try to do it on your own? All high achievers invest at least 10 percent of their gross income on personal development. When you decide to prepare to win, than a winner you will be.

What did you learn from this lesson? _____

_____

_____

_____

_____

_____

What action will you take today? _____

_____

_____

_____

_____

What are you grateful for after reading this lesson? _____

_____

_____

_____

_____

_____

www.ingramcontent.com/pod-product-compliance
Lightning Source LLC
Chambersburg PA
CBHW060354190526
45169CB00002B/590